SOMEONE ONCE TOLD ME I'M A BIT LIKE A CAT...
...SINCE I DON'T OPEN UP TO PEOPLE EASILY...
...AND TEND TO PREFER TO BE ON MY OWN.
I GUESS YOU COULD SAY THAT. IT'S NOT EXACTLY WRONG.
BUT ONE DAY...
...I WENT TO THE SECOND FLOOR OF THE GYM TO GET SOME TIME ALONE...
...AND STUMBLED UPON...
...ANOTHER CAT, QUIETLY HIDING IN THE SHADOWS.

Chapter 1: Ping-Pong in Blazers and Skirts

KAKON (PLUNK)
カコン
KAKON
カコン
KAKON
カコン
KAKON
カコン
SHIMA-MURA...
...YOU'VE GOTTEN PRETTY GOOD AT THIS.

I GUESS SKIPPING ALL THOSE CLASSES FINALLY PAID OFF.
THAT'S NOT SOMETHING TO BE PROUD OF...
LOOK WHO'S TALKING. YOU SKIP EVEN MORE THAN ME, ADACHI.
TRUE.
YET SOMEHOW THE TEACHERS STILL LIKE YOU BETTER.
WELL...
YOU DO DYE YOUR HAIR...
...AND WEAR EARRINGS.
HMPH...

BUT YOU'RE LIKE THREE TIMES THE SLACKER I AM.
YET HERE YOU ARE, CUTTING CLASS JUST LIKE ME.
SU (SHF)
スッ…
KOTEN (FLOP)
こてん

WHAT'S WRONG?
UMM...
THINGS WERE REALLY BUSY AT WORK YESTERDAY.
HIRA (WAVE)
ひら
HIRA
ひら
HUH, I DIDN'T KNOW YOU HAD A PART-TIME JOB.
HOW MATURE.
YEAH, I GUESS.
I DON'T KNOW MUCH AT ALL ABOUT ADACHI.
I MET HER JUST A FEW MONTHS AGO, AND WE ONLY SEE EACH OTHER...
... HERE IN THE GYM ANYWAY.
IT FEELS LIKE I'VE JUST SCRATCHED THE SURFACE...
...AND SHE'S STILL MOSTLY A MYSTERY TO ME.
THOUGH I GUESS THERE'S NOT REALLY A REASON FOR ME TO LEARN MORE ABOUT HER.

SURU (SLIP)
スルッ
THAT'S JUST THE KIND OF "FRIENDS" WE ARE. NOTHING MORE, NOTHING LESS.
YOUR SKIRT SMELLS LIKE YOU.
WHA— IS MY B.O. THAT BAD?
THAT'S NOT WHAT I MEANT...

YOU TAKE THINGS TOO LITERALLY, SHIMAMURA.
LITERALLY? HMM, LITERALLY, HUH...
I'VE NEVER HEARD THAT ONE BEFORE.
HEY, ADACHI.
HM?
WHY DON'T WE GO TO CLASS TOGETHER IN THE AFTERNOON?
......
WHAT'S WRONG?

NOTHING, JUST THINKING ABOUT OUR ATTEN-DANCE RECORD ...
UH, I MEAN...
...IT'D BE MORE FUN IF WE MAKE IT TO SECOND YEAR TOGETHER, RIGHT?
OHH.
YEAH.
I GUESS IT WON'T HURT TO SHOW MY FACE.
パタッ
PATA (FLOP)

OR DO YOU HAVE PLANS TO HANG OUT WITH SOMEONE?
NOT TODAY.
ACTUALLY, I PRETTY MUCH NEVER DO.
OH YEAH?
FINE, THEN...
...LET'S GO SOMEWHERE AFTER CLASS.
THEN HOW ABOUT WE GO TO WHERE YOU WORK?
HARD PASS...

SO, HOW DID IT FEEL TO BE BACK IN CLASS AFTER SO LONG?
HISTORY WAS FINE...
...BUT I HAD ZERO CLUE WHAT WAS GOING ON IN MATH.
I KNOW, RIGHT?
EVERYONE WAS STARING AT YOU, SHIMA-MURA.
WELL, NEITHER OF US IS EVER THERE, AND THEN WE BOTH SHOW UP OUT OF NOWHERE.
I BET THEY WERE LOOKING AT YOU TOO, ADACHI.
NO...
THEY WERE FOCUSED ON YOU.

MUST BE 'COS YOU'RE SO PRETTY.
!?
ガクッ
GAKU (SLIP)
AGH!
ぐらっ‥
GURA (WOBBLE)
WH—
WHOA!

ARE YOU PRETENDING THE STAIRS ARE LAVA OR SOMETHING?
HMPH.
YOU THREW ME OFF. NO ONE'S EVER CALLED ME PRETTY BEFORE.
TA
HUH.
TA (TMP)
......
NOT EVEN YOUR BOY-FRIEND?
I'VE NEVER HAD ONE.
HUH.

THEY MUST ALL BE BLIND.
YOU SURE IT'S NOT THE OTHER WAY AROUND?
YOU'RE THE WEIRD ONE, ADACHI.
KII (CREAK)
SO, WHERE DO YOU WANNA GO?

I'M GETTING A LITTLE HUNGRY.
I DIDN'T HAVE LUNCH.
OKAY, SO HOW 'BOUT WE GRAB SOMETHING TO EAT?
I'M KINDA IN THE MOOD FOR A DONUT.
DONUTS...
THE CLOSEST SHOP IS BY THE STATION.
TON (TAP)
TON
ALL RIGHT, LET'S GO.
WAIT...
WHERE'S YOUR BIKE?

I DIDN'T RIDE IT TODAY. IT'S GETTING REPAIRED AT THE SHOP.
WOW, SO YOU WALKED ALL THE WAY TO SCHOOL? THAT'S KINDA FAR.
PRETTY RESPONSIBLE FOR A DELINQUENT.
...I THOUGHT MAYBE YOU'D BE HERE.
HM?

SO BASICALLY, "I CAME TO SCHOOL...
"...TO SEE YOU"?
WHAT'S GOING ON...?

......
ガヤ
GAYA (GAB)
GAYA
ガヤ
IT'S SUPER POPULAR, HUH?
BUT I LOVE HOW SWEET IT SMELLS HERE.
I TOTALLY GET WHY BUGS GO FOR FLOWERS.
UHH, YEAH...I'M NOT TRYING TO THINK ABOUT THAT.

SHIMAMURA, WHAT ARE YOU GETTING?
IT'S ALWAYS SO HARD TO CHOOSE, BUT PROBABLY A FRENCH CRULLER.
I'M ALSO GONNA GET A COUPLE MORE FOR MY LITTLE SISTER.
YOU'RE GOING FOR THE FRENCH CRULLER TOO?
HM? THAT A PROBLEM?
I DON'T WANT TO GET THE SAME ONE AS YOU.
WHAT'S WRONG WITH THAT? JUST GET IT.
HMM...
NO, I'M GONNA GO WITH THIS ONE.

SHIMAMURA, ARE YOU GONNA GO TO CLASS AGAIN TOMORROW?
YEAH, I KINDA WANT TO SEE HOW LONG I CAN KEEP IT UP FOR.
I SEE.
スッ
SU (LEAN)
WHY DON'T WE TRY DOING OUR BEST...
...ADACHI-SAN?
OKAY, BUT JUST A LITTLE.

WANT A BITE?
SURE, THANKS.
OKAY, YOUR TURN. TRY MINE.
HERE.

......
OHH, I GET IT.
じっ…
JI (STARE)
SORRY.
THE CREAM'S THE BEST PART, RIGHT?
HERE, TAKE IT.

IF YOU SAY SO...
PAKU (CHOMP)
パク
COME TO THINK OF IT, I GET THE FEELING...
...ONE OF MY REPORT CARDS BACK IN ELEMENTARY SCHOOL...
...SAID I WAS "AN ABSENT-MINDED CHILD."
I LOVE THOSE MOMENTS...
...WHEN I CAN JUST LET GO AND LAZE AROUND.

BUT IT GETS HARDER TO DO THAT IF I'M WITH SOMEONE ELSE.
MAYBE THAT'S WHY...
...I PREFER BEING ON MY OWN AFTER ALL.
SHIMA-MURA?
OH, UHH...
SHOULD WE GET GOING?

WHERE SHOULD WE GO?
IF I WERE ALONE, I COULD JUST WALK AROUND WHEREVER I FELT LIKE...
...AND GO HOME WHENEVER I GOT TIRED, BUT...
...ADACHI'S HERE NOW.
THIS IS EXACTLY WHY IT'S SORT OF PAINFUL...
...TO BE AROUND PEOPLE...
THEY CAN BE A PAIN TO DEAL WITH...
THEY'RE HARD TO UNDER-STAND...
AND WHEN THINGS GET ROCKY, YOU HAVE TO FIND A WAY TO MAKE UP.

BUT I GUESS IT'S IN BETWEEN PUTTING UP WITH THOSE DOWNSIDES...
...THAT YOU CAN STUMBLE UPON HAPPY MEMORIES...
...LIKE WHEN YOU'RE A KID...
...AND YOU SUDDENLY FIND A SMALL BALL YOU HAD LOST.
I WANT TO BELIEVE MEETING ADACHI...
...IS IN ITSELF A STEP TOWARD A BRIGHTER FUTURE...

UM...
IF YOU DON'T LIKE IT, I'LL LET GO.
RIGHT AWAY.
NO, YOU JUST SURPRISED ME...
SHOULD I STOP?
KYU (CLASP)
...NO, IT'S FINE.
LET'S GO.

GYU (SQUEEZE)
ぎゅっ
ADACHI, ARE YOU SECRETLY THE TYPE WHO LIKES TO BE PAMPERED?
NO, I'M...
...NOT.

きゅう
KYUU (CLASP)
IT JUST DOESN'T SEEM LIKE YOU.
IT FEELS PRETTY NORMAL... TO ME.
HAS ADACHI ALWAYS GONE AROUND...
...HOLDING PEOPLE'S HANDS LIKE THIS?
I WONDER IF SHE FINDS IT COMFORTING.
IT'S NOT LIKE SHE'S INTO GIRLS OR ANYTHING...
...PROBABLY.
RIGHT...?

ピク
PIKU (TWITCH)
WHAT WOULD I DO IF ADACHI...
...CAME OUT AND SAID SHE HAD A CRUSH ON ME?
ぎゅっ
GYU (SQUEEZE)
SERIOUSLY, WHAT WOULD I ACTUALLY DO?

SHIMAMURA, WHERE ARE YOU GOING?
HUH?
NOWHERE, REALLY.
GOT ANY PLACE IN MIND, ADACHI?
I'M GOOD WITH ANYWHERE YOU WANT TO GO.
THIS IS TOUGH. WHERE SHOULD WE GO?
SHOPPING, MAYBE...?
NOPE. I DON'T KNOW WHY, BUT...
...THAT FEELS WAY OFF...
BIKU (JUMP)
SHIMA-MURA?
!?
BA (TURN)

I KNEW IT WAS YOU!
PAAA (BEAM)
WE WENT TO MIDDLE SCHOOL TOGETHER, REMEMBER?
OHH, YEAH! WHAT A COINCI-DENCE.
LONG TIME NO SEE.

I ALMOST COULDN'T TELL IT WAS YOU 'COS YOUR HAIR'S SO MUCH LIGHTER.
YOU LOOK KINDA LIKE A DROPOUT.
HA-HA-HA, I GET THAT A LOT.
I DIDN'T THINK I'D RUN INTO YOU HERE.
OH, I KNOW, WHY DON'T WE EXCHANGE NUMBERS WHILE WE'RE AT IT?
OKAY, SURE.
SHIMAMURA.
ビクッ
BIKU (FLINCH)
I'M GONNA GO GET MY BIKE.
WHA—?

BUT SHE DIDN'T RIDE HER BIKE IN TODAY.
OH, MAYBE SHE'S GOING TO PICK IT UP AT THE SHOP?
THIS IS ME.
SEE YOU TOMORROW.
HEEEY!
KURU (SPIN)
くるっ
...SHE'S NOT ANGRY, IS SHE?

DID SHE GET PISSED 'COS I WASN'T PAYING ATTENTION TO HER?
NO, THAT CAN'T BE IT.
I DON'T GET YOU AT ALL, ADACHI.
ハァ…
HAA (SIGH)
I KNEW IT— SPENDING TIME WITH SOMEONE IS SO MUCH WORK.
MAYBE I'M NOT CUT OUT FOR IT.

ADACHI, TRYING HER BEST TO STAY COOL
(AND NOT NECESSARILY SUCCEEDING)

Adachi and Shimamura

I HAD A DREAM...
...I KISSED SHIMAMURA.

AARGH!
UUGH!
ぐしゃ
GUSHA (RUFFLE)
ぐしゃ
GUSHA
I MEAN, I'M NOT EVEN A... YOU KNOW...!
AND SHIMA-MURA'S DEFINITELY NOT...
そっ...
SO (BRUSH)

IT DIDN'T FEEL LIKE ANYTHING WHEN HER LIPS MET MINE.
I'VE NEVER EVEN TOUCHED THEM...
...SO THERE'S NO WAY I'D KNOW WHAT THEY'RE LIKE.
SURU (SLIP)
するっ
BUT...
...HER FINGERS FELT EXACTLY AS SOFT AS THEY WERE IN REAL LIFE—

AAAGH!!
ボフ
BOFU (WHAP)
ボフ
BOFU
ボフ
BOFU
ボフ
BOFU
ばふっ
BAFU (POOMF)
IT'S PROBABLY JUST A SIGN...
...I WANT TO GET CLOSER TO HER AS A FRIEND.
IT DOESN'T REALLY MEAN ANYTHING.
ドキ
DOKI (BADUM)
ドキ
DOKI
ガヤ
GAYA (GAB)
ガヤ
GAYA
LET'S GET OUR LUNCHES.
'KAY.

DID YOU BRING YOURS?
I DIDN'T HAVE TIME TO MAKE IT...
WHAT DOES SHIMAMURA ACTUALLY THINK OF ME?
HOW CLOSE OF A FRIEND AM I TO HER?
OKAY, THEN LET'S GO TO THE CAFETERIA.
GATA (CLAK)
ガタ

I DON'T WANT TO BE WITH ANYONE IF IT MEANS I HAVE TO READ INTO WHAT THEY WANT ALL THE TIME.
I THINK MAYBE SHIMAMURA SENSED THAT...
...SO SHE NEVER FORCES ME INTO ANYTHING, BUT...
GA (SCOOT) ガ
GA ガ
GA ガ
SU (SHF) スッ
...THAT'S WHY I WANT HER TO LEAVE HER OTHER FRIENDS AT MOMENTS LIKE THIS...
...AND COME BE WITH ME.

YEAH.
I JUST WANT HER TO PUT ME FIRST. THAT'S ALL.
I WANT TO BE THE FIRST THING SHE THINKS OF...
...WHEN SHE HEARS THE WORD "FRIEND."

INESE
UMM...
WHY AM I THE ONLY ONE WHO HAS TO WEAR A CHINESE DRESS...?
キッパリ KIPPARI (BLUNT)
'COS YOU'RE YOUNG, OF COURSE.
THAT MAKES NO SENSE...
ピッ PI (TUG)

GU (STRETCH)
GU
I HOPE WE DON'T GET TOO BUSY TODAY.
PA (FLICK)
ガラ
GARA (SLIDE)
WELCO—
OH...

OH.

OOOH.
JIRO
JIRO (STARE)
DARA
DARA (FIDGET)
DARA
DARA
......
......
WOOOW.
KAAA (BLUUUSH)

FRIEND OF YOURS?
JI (STARE)
じっ…
YEAH, FROM SCHOOL.
PEKO (BOW)
ペコッ
A CHINESE DRESS, HUH?
SO THIS IS WHERE YOU WORK.
ぐぬ…
GUNU (IRK)
....
PARTY OF FOUR.
THIS WAY, PLEASE.
コッ
KO (TNK)

じっ…
JI (STARE)
コソッ
KOSO (WHISPER)
THIS IS WHY I DIDN'T WANT YOU TO COME HERE.
WHY NOT? IT LOOKS GOOD ON YOU.
SA (SHF)

ずいっ
ZUI (LEAN)
ADACHI-CHAN, WAS IT?
HMPH.
YES.
SO YOU'RE FRIENDS, HUUUH?
ペラ
PERA (BLAB)
YOU KNOW, ONCE YOU GIRLS HIT HIGH SCHOOL, FRIENDS STOP COMING OVER TO VISIT AT THE HOUSE...
ペラ
PERA
...SO I DON'T REALLY KNOW WHO MY LITTLE GIRL'S HANGING OUT WITH NOW.
?
?
AARGH, COME ON!
IT'S FINE. FORGET IT.
DON'T LISTEN TO HER.
BISHI (THRUST)
ビシッ

ARE YOU IN THE SAME CLASS?
DROP IT!
WHAAAT?
SHI SHI (SHOO)
UM... SO...
...PLEASE LET ME KNOW WHEN YOU'RE READY TO ORDER.
OKAAAY!
TA (TMP)
TA
TA
TA
TA
TA
SIIIGH...
I CAN'T BELIEVE I HAVE TO KEEP WEARING THIS IN FRONT OF SHIMAMURA...

どよっ…
DOYO (GLOOM)
KILL ME NOW...
IS SHE A FRIEND?
A FRIEND...
KOKUN (NOD)
コクン

GYO (SHOCK)
THE SHARK FIN'S SOOO EXPENSIVE!
HA HA HA!
DON'T GET THAT.
WOW, IT REALLY IS.
FRIED CHICKEN!
THEY'RE SO CLOSE...
...NOTHING LIKE MY FAMILY.

ドキッ
DOKI (BADUM)

I'M SURE TO SHIMAMURA ...
...IT MUST LOOK LIKE I'M JUST EMBARRASSED ABOUT WEARING THIS DRESS, BUT...
BO (FLUSH)
I SWEAR THERE WAS NOTHING DIRTY ABOUT THAT...!

IT'S JUST HARD TO KNOW HOW CLOSE TO GET TO HER...
...AND THOSE WORRIES SHOWED UP IN MY DREAM.
THAT'S ALL.
I CAN'T SAY I'D HATE TO TRY IT.
BUT IT'S NOT LIKE I'M DYING TO EITHER.
ADACHI-CHAN!
GO ON.
TON (PAT)

BUT IF THE TABLES WERE TURNED ...
...AND SHIMAMURA TRIED TO KISS ME...
...I KNOW FOR SURE I WOULDN'T TURN HER DOWN.

BOOO (DAZE)
ぼーー…
IT'S BEEN A WEEK SINCE I LAST CUT CLASS.

MAYBE SHIMAMURA WILL NOTICE I'M NOT THERE...
...AND COME CHECK ON ME.
WAIT, THAT MAKES ME...
...NO BETTER THAN A SPOILED BRAT WHO WANTS SOME-ONE TO FUSS OVER THEM.
HAAH.
AM I THE ONLY ONE...
...WHO CAN'T STOP THINKING ABOUT HOW WE SAW EACH OTHER YESTERDAY...?

I'M GETTING SO WORKED UP ALL ON MY OWN.
IS THERE SOMETHING WRONG WITH ME?
EVERYTHING I DO IS STARTING TO REVOLVE AROUND HER.
IT'S ALMOST LIKE I'VE GOT A ONE-SIDED CRUSH ON HER OR SOMETHING ...
PETA (STEP)
PETA

GACHA (CLAK)
カチ
ADACHI.
......
YEAH?
HOW ABOUT YOU COME TO THE CAFETERIA WITH ME FOR A CHANGE?
SU (SHF)
スッ
OKAY, SURE...

JUST AS I WAS STARTING TO THINK SHE'D TURNED A CORNER, SHE'S GONE AND DONE IT AGAIN.
WHO'RE YOU SUPPOSED TO BE?
OUR HOMEROOM TEACHER.
I WAS ASKED ABOUT WHAT WAS UP WITH YOU TODAY, BUT HOW SHOULD I KNOW?
THE TEACHER ASKED SHIMAMURA ABOUT ME.
THAT MEANS...

...OUR HOMEROOM TEACHER MUST THINK SHIMAMURA AND I ARE CLOSE.
CLOSE ENOUGH TO ASK HER BEFORE ANYONE ELSE.
HUH.
WAS IT THAT FUNNY?
I DON'T THINK MY IMPRESSION WAS VERY GOOD.
HUH? WHAT DO YOU MEAN?

ニッコリ
NIKKORI (SMILE)
THAT FACE.
?
ハッ
HA (GASP)
ムニ
MUNI (SQUISH)
ムニ
MUNI
ムニ
MUNI

YOU DON'T HAVE TO GET THAT EMBARRASSED ABOUT IT.
EASIER SAID THAN DONE.

Adachi and Shimamura

Chapter 3: The Adachi Question 2

ガヤ
GAYA (GAB)
LET'S DIG...
...IN...
GAYA
ガヤ
JIII (STARE)
じ
WHAT?
HEH HEH.
I WAS JUST THINKING YOU LOOKED SO CUTE IN THAT DRESS YESTERDAY.
ACK!
YOU'RE CUTE TOO, YOU KNOW?

BUT I'M NOT DOING ANYTHING SPECIAL. I ALWAYS LOOK LIKE THIS.
MY POINT EXACTLY. YOU ALWAYS LOOK CUTE.
IT'S BEEN A WHILE...
...SINCE I GOT TO TALK WITH SHIMAMURA, JUST THE TWO OF US...
SHIMA-MURAAA!
HEY, HEY!
OH.

UMM...
HI, ...-SAN.
HER NAME'S ADACHI.
YOU THOUGHT YOU COULD GET AWAY WITH FOR-GETTING HER NAME IF YOU MUMBLED, DIDN'T YOU?
KACHA (CLAK)
OH, COME ON. IT'S NO BIG DEAL.
PEKO (BOW)
MY NAME'S HINO.
I'M NAKAFUJI.
BUT MAYBE YOU KNOW SINCE WE'RE ALL IN THE SAME CLASS.
THEY'RE NOT TRYING TO EAT WITH US...ARE THEY?
PACHIN (SNAP)
THANKS FOR THE MEAL.
I GUESS THAT'S A YES.

I'M SURPRISED TO SEE YOU TWO HERE. DON'T YOU NORMALLY BRING YOUR OWN LUNCH?
MY MOM OVERSLEPT THIS MORNING.
I DIDN'T HAVE ANYTHING I COULD PACK FOR LUNCH.
MAKES SENSE.
HYOI (LIFT)
I DON'T WANT THIS.
SO LAST SUNDAY...
...I MET THIS SUPER WEIRD KID AT THE FISHING POND.

DON'T GIVE ME YOUR SCRAPS.
OH YEAH? WEIRD HOW?
SHE WAS PROBABLY IN LIKE, ELEMENTARY SCHOOL, BUT SHE HAD THIS CRAZY SPACE SUIT ON...
...AND WAS GOING AROUND LIKE "KUHH-HOO, KUH-HOO."
WHAAT? A SPACE SUIT?
SHIMAMURA, DO YOU WANNA MEET HER? SHE'S KIND OF HILARIOUS.
NICE TRY. YOU JUST WANT ME TO GO FISHING WITH YOU, RIGHT?
NO, NO, THAT'S JUST AN ADDED BONUS.
BUT I TOLD HER A BIT ABOUT YOU AND SHE SAID SHE WANTED TO MEET YOU.
WHAT EXACTLY DID YOU TELL HER ABOUT ME...?
I SAID CUT THAT OUT.
ス
SU (SHF)

WHY DON'T YOU JUST TAKE NAKAFUJI?
CAN'T, I HAVE A CLUB MEETING.
SEE? C'MON, SHIMAMURA, LET'S GOOO!
UGHH...

ADACHI, WHAT'RE YOU GONNA DO FOR AFTERNOON CLASSES?
I FIGURED I'D GO.
GASHA (CLATTER)
ガシャ
OH YEAH?
HEY...
HM?

COULD I GO OVER TO YOUR PLACE TODAY?
......
WHY?
I DON'T HAVE ANYTHING ELSE TO DO...
I MEAN...
...I JUST FEEL LIKE IT.
?
THERE'S NOT MUCH TO DO THERE.
AND MY LITTLE SISTER IS...
I MEAN, I GUESS IT'S OKAY.

BUT I'M TELLING YOU, THERE'S REALLY NOTHING TO DO.
OKAY.
ALL THAT MATTERS IS THE FACT...
...THAT I'VE BEEN TO HER HOUSE.
I JUST WANT TO FEEL ONE STEP CLOSER TO HER...
...AND THAT MUCH MORE SPECIAL THAN EVERYONE ELSE.

HERE WE ARE AT THE SHIMAMURAS'...
DON (BAM)
DON'T TALK TO YOURSELF LIKE THAT. YOU SOUND LIKE HINO.
NO WAAAY.
ドキ
DOKI (BADUM)
ドキ
DOKI
DOKI
ドキ
EXCUSE ME...
YOUR ROOM'S ON THE FIRST FLOOR?
YEAH, WHY?
I GUESS BEDROOMS ARE USUALLY ON THE SECOND FLOOR, HUH?
IT'S HERE.

GACHA (OPEN)
ONEE-CHAN, WELCOME...
PAA (BEAM)
...BACK.
I'M HOME.
OH, THIS IS MY FRIEND. SHE'S THE ONE WE SAW WORKING AT THE CHINESE RESTAURANT YESTERDAY.
PEKO (BOW)
YEAH.
PI (BOOP)
TA (STEP)
TA
I FEEL KINDA BAD.
OH, DON'T. SHE CAN BE A LITTLE SHY.

COME ON IN.
THERE'S TWO DESKS SIDE BY SIDE...
...AND TWO SETS OF FUTONS.
THIS SHOULD'VE BEEN GLARINGLY OBVIOUS, BUT...
...IT'S TOTALLY DIFFERENT FROM THE ROOM I SAW IN MY DREAM.

BAFU (POOMF)
HERE.
...SO, WHAT SHOULD WE DO?
....
....

SNAP OUT OF IT. THAT WAS JUST A DREAM.
BUT...
...UM!
SHIMAMURA ...
HMM?

UM...
WOULD IT BE OKAY...
...IF I MAYBE...
...SAT...
... BETWEEN YOUR LEGS?
UH...
WH- WHAT THE HELL AM I SAYING...!?
I'M MUTTERING LIKE A TOTAL CREEP—
KERO (BLURT)
OKAY.
HOW IS THAT OKAY?

GO AHEAD.
...WAIT, WHAT?
WHAT THE WHAT?
AM I STILL DREAMING...?
......
ドッ
DO (THUMP)
ドッ
DO
I-IS...
...IS THIS REALLY OKAY?
ジリ
JIRI (INCH)
ドッ
DO
ドッ
DO
SHE REALLY DOESN'T MIND...!?
ドッ
DO

ジリ…
JIRI (CRAWL)
ちょこん・・
CHOKON (PLOP)
WHOA...
WHOA!

PURU (TREMBLE)
PURU
WHAT ARE YOU DOING?
NOTHING! JUST—
HM? MY SISTER SITS CLOSE LIKE THIS ALL THE TIME.
IS IT WEIRD?
SH-SHE'S TREATING ME LIKE HER SISTER...
...WELL, I GUESS THAT'S FINE FOR NOW.
N—
NO, IT'S NORMAL, I GUESS.
NORMAL?
IS THIS ACTUALLY PRETTY NORMAL?
SERIOUSLY?

HYUP!
GUI
(PULL)
AH!
TON
(SHNK)

WAIT ...
...IS THIS ACTUALLY A DREAM?
GYU (PINCH)
OW, OUCH.
NOPE, IT'S REAL LIFE...
H-HEY, UM...
DO YOU HAVE LIKE...
...A BOY-FRIEND?
KAAAA (BLUSH)
WHAT DO YOU THINK?
NO...
GOOD GUESS.
ACTUALLY, I TOLD YOU THE OTHER DAY THAT I DON'T.
OH, REALLY ...?

HOW ABOUT YOU, ADACHI? DATING ANYONE?
NO.
I SEE.
SHE JUST ASKED ME BACK TO BE POLITE.
IT'S NOT LIKE SHE'S INTERESTED IN ME.
NO MATTER HOW HARD I TRY TO BE SOMEONE SPECIAL TO SHIMAMURA...
...MY INTENTIONS NEVER GET THROUGH TO HER.

I FEEL LIKE WE'VE EACH GOT OUR OWN MIS-MATCHED RULERS...
...SO THE WAY WE MEASURE THINGS BETWEEN US NEVER LINES UP.
IT'S LIKE NOTHING EITHER OF US DOES...
...IS EVER ENOUGH TO CLOSE THE GAP.
IS THIS HOW IT'S ALWAYS GOING TO BE?

KURU (FWIP)
I LIKE YOU, SHIMAMURA ...!!
SHI... ......!!
HA (GASP)
HUH? WHAA—?
WHAT WAS I GOING TO SAY?
WAIT, DID I SAY IT? DID I STOP?
WHAT WOULD HAPPEN IF SHE KNEW?
?

...SHI—
I KINDA LIKE YOU, SHIMAMURA.
BIKU (FLINCH)
ビクッ
... SHIMA —
YURA (SWAY)
ゆらっ
I PROB... ...LI—
I...I THINK I LIKE YOU, MAYBE? I MEAN, THIS IS JUST A MAYBE, BUT...
...I-IT'S LIKE I'M INTO YOU? OR WHATEVER...
NOPE.
THIS ISN'T GONNA WORK.
I'M SUCH AN IDIOT!

THIS... THIS IS...
...THE DUMBEST THING I COULD DO!
UMM, ARE YOU ALL RIGHT? YOU BREATHING OKAY? YOUR FACE IS SUPER RED...

BA (JUMP)
WHA—
HEY ...!
BATAN (SLAM)
WHAT JUST HAPPENED?
W-WAIT...

ガシャッ
GASHA (CLANG)
ダダダダ
DA (DASH)
DA
DA
DA
バフッ
BAFU (FWUMP)
YOU BLEW IT, SHTOOPID!

I'M SHO SHTOOPID ...
UUGH... WAAA...
WAA HAA...
AAAGH ...
KOFF! KOFF! KOFF...

PATA (FLOP)
パタ
WHAT AM I DOING?
WHAAAT AM I DOOOING?

TAKE THAT!
EEEK!
DO (BAM)
DO
DO

Adachi and Shimamura

HUH?
WHAT? DID SHE JUST LEAVE?
WHY?
IT LOOKED LIKE SHE WAS TRYING REALLY HARD TO TELL ME SOMETHING...
IS IT SOMETHING DIFFICULT TO SAY?
WHAT COULD BE THAT BAD...?
FOR EXAMPLE......
HMM......

NAH, NO WAY.
ガチャ
GACHA (CLAK)
SHABA-DABAAA!
SHE'S GONE.
GOOD.
ストン
SUTON (SHUNK)
SHE LEFT PRETTY QUICK, HUH?
YEAH.
DID YOU GUYS FIIIGHT?
HMM...
I'M NOT REALLY SURE MYSELF.

Chapter 4: Isosceles Triangle

キーンコーン
KIIIN (DING)
KOOON (DONG)
SHIMA-MUU!
IS ADACHI NOT COMIN' TO SCHOOL TODAY?
I DON'T THINK SHE'S HERE.
WHY ARE YOU ASKING ME?
I THOUGHT MAYBE YOU'D KNOW.
IT'S HER TURN FOR DAY DUTY.
?
OUR HOMEROOM TEACHER DID THE SAME THING.
THANKS ANYWAY!
You okaaay? Or whatever??
10:45
WHY IS EVERYONE ASKING ME...?
NO ANSWER...

IT'S ALREADY LUNCH, YOU KNOW...
コト
KOTO (TNK)
WHY WON'T ADACHI ANSWER ME...?
You okaaay? Or
10:45
IS SHE JUST IGNORING ME?
ポチ
POCHI (CLIK)
NO, MAYBE SHE HASN'T EVEN SEEN IT.
THAT'S PROBABLY IT, BUT...
......
......
......I GUESS I CAN GO CHECK ON HER.

GOOD THING I MANAGED TO GET HER ADDRESS OUT OF HER THE OTHER DAY...
PERA (FWIP)
10:45
You okaaay? Or whateve
PA (POP)
I'm thinking about going to your house later. Is that cool?
AAAND SENT.
MOGU (MUNCH)
MOGU
CHUUU (SLUUURP)
10:45
You okaaay? Or whatever??
12:16
I'm thinking about going to your house later. Is that cool?
SHIIIN (SILENT)
OKAY.
I'M JUST GONNA GO.

HAAH...
I CAN'T HELP BUT THINK GETTING CLOSE TO SOMEONE SHOULD HAPPEN NATURALLY.
IT SHOULDN'T BE SOMETHING YOU HAVE TO WORK SO HARD AT...
GREETINGS, SHIMAMURA-SAN.
HUH?

どん
DON (BAM)
YOU ARE SHIMAMURA-SAN, CORRECT?
シュコー
SHUKOOO (SHHHK)
シュコー
SHUKOOO
WHA—?
UH... EXCUSE ME, BUT WHO ARE YOU?

I KNEW IT! I WAS RIGHT!
MY NAME IS YASHIRO.
HINO-SAN TOLD ME ALL ABOUT YOU.
I RECOGNIZED YOUR HAIR COLOR AND THOUGHT IT MIGHT BE YOU.
SHUKOOO
SHUKOOO
HINO... OH!
SO THIS IS WHAT SHE MEANT BY A SPACE SUIT...
OH, YOU DO KNOW ABOUT ME!
GOSO (RATTLE)
JUST A MOMENT, PLEASE...

PASA (FWIP)
I FINALLY HAD A FACE MADE SO I THOUGHT I'D INTRODUCE MYSELF.
HOW DID IT TURN OUT?
HER HAIR...
...IS LIGHT BLUE...

YOU... HAD A FACE MADE?
EXACTLY. NICE TO MEET YOU TOO.
I MEAN, UM...NICE TO MEET YOU...
I FEEL A STRONG SENSE OF SHARED DESTINY WITH YOU.
I WONDER ABOUT THAT...
I BELIEVE YOU WERE ALMOST CERTAINLY BORN INTO THIS WORLD IN ORDER TO MEET ME.
HUH? I WAS BORN TO MEET YOU?

YES.
I IMAGINE WE WILL MEET AGAIN.
?
OOPS.
グゥゥゥゥ
GUUUU (GROOOWL)
I'D FORGOTTEN I WAS ON MY WAY TO PROCURE DINNER.
UNTIL WE MEET AGAAAIN!
TE て (TMP)
TE て
TE て
KUH-HOO. KUUH-HOOO.
WHAT IN THE WORLD WAS THAT...?

...I FEEL LIKE I ALREADY SAW THE MAIN EVENT...
...AND I HAVEN'T EVEN DONE ANYTHING YET...
PIN (DING)
ピンポーン
POON (DOOONG)
安達
SIGN: ADACHI
GACHA (CLAK)
ガチャ
YES?
YO.
KAAA (BLUSH)
カァァ
GIVE ME FIFTEEN MINUTES!
WHA—? THAT'S PRETTY LONG.
elephant
elephant

WHY DID YOU PUT YOUR UNIFORM ON?
DUNNO. JUST KINDA WENT WITH IT.
DON'T COME OVER ALL OF A SUDDEN LIKE THAT. YOU CAUGHT ME OFF GUARD.
I DIDN'T. I TOLD YOU I WAS COMING.
YOU TOLD ME?
I KNEW IT. YOU DIDN'T SEE MY MESSAGES, DID YOU?
OHH...
I COULDN'T. I FORGOT MY BAG AT YOUR HOUSE.
OH, IS THAT WHAT HAPPENED?
WHAT DID YOU TEXT ME?

JUST LIKE, "YOU OKAY?"
YEAH, I'M REAL GOOD!
I MISSED THAT. DO IT AGAIN?
NO WAY.
HEY, CAN I COME INSIDE?
IT'S KINDA AWKWARD STANDING AROUND OUT HERE.
UH...
IT'S JUST... I HAVE WORK TODAY.
OH, I SEE.
WELL, YOU LOOK OKAY, SO I GUESS I'LL HEAD BACK.
HUH? WHA—?

H-HEY! SHIMA-MURA...
HM?
DO YOU WANT TO GO ON A DA—
DO YOU WANT TO SPEND THE DAY TOGETHER SOMEWHERE?
LIKE, MAYBE SATURDAY? WE COULD GO ANYWHERE.
SPEND THE DAY? WHERE?
WHER-EVER...
GONYO (FIDGET)

WELL...... WHY NOT?
AS LONG AS YOU CHOOSE THE PLACE.
SURE!
COOL... THEN, HAVE FUN AT WORK.
...!
DA (STOMP)
だだだだだ
DA
DA
DA
SATURDAY, HUH...
I GUESS THIS'LL BE MY FIRST TIME HANGING OUT WITH ADACHI ON A WEEKEND.

OH.
KURU (FWIP)
WHERE'D YOU GET THAT ELEPHANT T-SHIRT?
NOT TELLING!
WAS ADACHI...
...ABOUT TO SAY "DATE"?
...NAH, THAT'S CRAZY.

ARE'NT YOU COLD?
NO, I CAN REGULATE MY BODY TEMPERATURE.

Adachi and Shimamura

HEY.
YOU MUST BE SHIMAMURA-SAN'S FRIEND.
NICE TO MEET YOU.
Chapter 5: Isosceles Triangle 2

WHA—
HUH? WHO'S THIS?
A LITTLE ALIEN I MET THE OTHER DAY.
WE RAN INTO EACH OTHER WHILE I WAS WAITING HERE.
PEKOOO (BOW)
WE KNEW NOT WE'D BOTH BE HERE, AND YET WE MET AGAIN.
OUR DESTINIES TRULY ARE LINKED!
GRR.

MAY I ASK YOUR NAME?
ADACHI.
AND WHO MIGHT YOU...
WHO... ARE YOU?
THE SHORT ANSWER IS AN INTERGALACTIC TRAVELER FROM THE FUTURE. HOWEVER...
...PLEASE FEEL FREE TO CALL ME YASHIRO CHIKAMA.
......
......
SHIMAMURA, TRANSLATE.
KURA (DIZZY)
IT MIGHT BE EASIER TO THINK OF HER AS...
...A QUIRKY GIRL FROM THE NEIGHBOR-HOOD.
PON (PAT)
PON
WELL THEN, SHALL WE?
PETA (STEP)
PETA
HUH?
PETA

YOU'RE COMING WITH US?
SOMETHING SMELLS DELICIOUS OVER THERE.
TA (TMP)
WAIT, WHAT THE HELL?
STAY CLOSE OR YOU'LL GET LOST!
TODAY WAS MEANT TO BE...
...MY DA— ...WITH SHIMAMURA ...

GYU
(GRAB)
!?
BIKU
(JUMP)
ビクッ
WH-
WHAT?

I THOUGHT YOU MIGHT RUN AWAY AGAIN.
HUH?
...OH.
WE ALREADY CAME ALL THE WAY HERE.
WHAT'S THE POINT IF YOU DITCH ME RIGHT OFF THE BAT?
I'M NOT GONNA DITCH YOU.
I'M SURE YOU'VE GOT A LOT OF QUESTIONS.
TRUST ME, I DO TOO.
BUT LET'S JUST GO AND SEE WHAT HAPPENS.

OH, AND...
...GOOD MORNING!
MORNING.

TABLE FOR THREE, PLEASE!
COME, SIT OVER HERE.
HUH? OH.
UMM.
HEH...
NIKOOO (SMILE)

...!?
JIII
(GLARE)
SHIMAMURA, SCOOCH IN A LITTLE MORE.
HUH?
UH, OKAY.
ストンッ
SUTON
(PLUNK)

....WAIT, WAIT, WAIT.
THIS IS ABSURD.
WHY ARE WE ALL SITTING ON THE SAME SIDE OF THE BOOTH?
WE LOOK LIKE WE'RE WAITING FOR SOMEONE TO COME JOIN US ON THE OTHER SIDE.
IT'S SUPER WEIRD.
SEE, EVEN THE SERVER LOOKS CONFUSED.
UMM, PLEASE LET ME KNOW WHEN YOU ARE READY TO PLACE YOUR ORDER.
THIS MEAL IS ON ME, SO PLEASE FEEL FREE TO ORDER ANYTHING YOU LIKE.
I'D LIKE THIS FLUFFY SOUFFLÉ OMELET.

ADACHI, WHAT ARE YOU GETTING?
CHOOSE WHATEVER STRIKES YOUR FANCY.
I CAN'T READ IT FROM THERE. CAN I SEE IT FOR A SEC?
YOU GOT IT.
CHEZ MADU
CHEZ MADU
SHIMAMURA, WHICH ARE YOU GOING FOR?
YEAH, WHAT SHOULD I GET...?
CHEZ MADU

HOW ABOUT WE ORDER PASTA AND A PIZZA AND SPLIT THEM?
SURE.
GURI (TICKLE)
GURI
GURI
GAH!

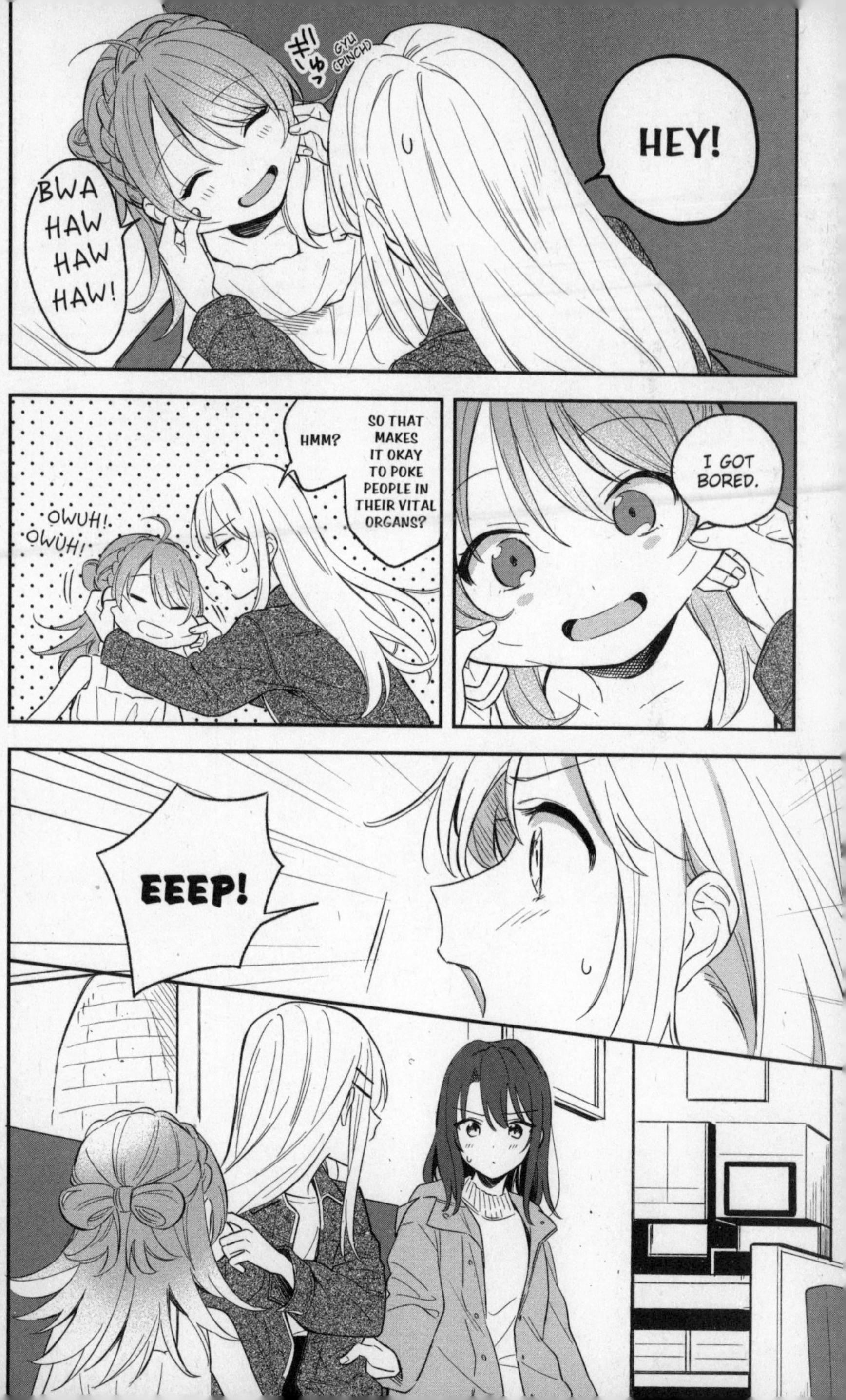
HEY!
ぎゅっ
GYU (PINCH)
BWA HAW HAW HAW!
I GOT BORED.
HMM?
SO THAT MAKES IT OKAY TO POKE PEOPLE IN THEIR VITAL ORGANS?
OWUH! OWUH!
EEEP!

WHAAAT? WHY ARE YOU BOTH SO FIXATED ON MY LOVE HANDLES?
I REAAALLY DON'T APPRECIATE THAT KIND OF ATTENTION.
YOU CHOOSE THE PIZZA.
AND I'LL CHOOSE THE PASTA.
OWIEEE.
OKAY, THIS ONE.
MARGHERITA ¥700
MARINARA
BACON AND ZUCCHINI ¥900
THEN I'LL GET THIS ONE.

SHIN
(SILENCE)
HEH-HEH. HOW DO YOU LIKE MY GRASS-HOPPER?
......

EVEN I CAN DO THAT.
OOH, A CHOPSTICK STAND.
IT'S ALMOST THE SAME AS YOURS, THOUGH.
HOW EXACTLY?
DOESN'T MINE LOOK MORE GRASSHOPPER-LIKE?
NEITHER OF THEM LOOK LIKE A GRASSHOPPER TO ME.
AHHH, YOU EARTHLINGS...
...YOU HAVE NO ARTISTIC SENSIBILITY.

ADACHI.
WHAT'S WRONG?
N—
NOTHING...
FUEEEH...
THEN SMILE FOR ME AND DO THAT THING AGAIN.
WH-WHAT THING?
THAT THING FROM THE OTHER DAY. OKAY, HERE I GO.
YOU OKAAAY?
WHAA...?

I...I'M REAL GOOD!
BA (DUCK)
YOU KNOW, IT'S HARD TO READ PEOPLE'S MINDS.
YOU NEVER REALLY KNOW WHAT MAKES THEM UPSET OR WHAT THEY WANT.
BUT IF YOU'RE ALREADY TOGETHER, WHY NOT TRY TO HAVE A LITTLE FUN?
THAT'S HOW I SEE IT.
I WISH YOU WOULD TOO.

だばーっ
DABAAA (SPLOOSH)
IT'S SUPER SOFT AND PILLOWY!
ぷわ
PUWA (FLUFF)
WHOAAA, SO FLUFFY!
ぷわ
PUWA
MMMMM!
GIVE ME A BITE.
OF COURSE.

HERE YOU GOOO.
SAY "AAAH."
WHA—!?
WHAT'S WRONG? DID YOU WANT SOME TOO?
NOT EXACTLY...

WOULD YOU PLEASE HURRY UP?
ALL RIGHT, ALL RIGHT.
WHO EVEN TALKS LIKE THAT?
NOT THAT PART. I WANT SOME WITH THE FRENCH BREAD.
YOU'RE PRETTY DEMANDING, AREN'T YOU, SHIMAMURA-SAN?
SO THEY TELL ME.
SO SWEET! I THINK YOU PUT TOO MUCH SYRUP ON IT.
DO YOU THINK SO?
GYU (SQUEEZE)

I TOLD YOU, ADACHI, STOP PINCHING MY STOMACH.
YEAH, SURE. LET ME GIVE YOU A BITE OF MY PASTA TOO.
HUH? WEREN'T WE GOING TO SPLIT IT?
I KNOW, BUT THIS ONE'S EXTRA.
WHAT DOES THAT EVEN MEAN?
I WONDER IF ADACHI'S HANG-UP WITH YASHIRO...
...ISN'T THAT SHE HATES HER, BUT FEELS A KIND OF RIVALRY?
PAKU (CHOMP)

JI (STARE)
ADACHI IS ACTUALLY...
...A LOT MORE CHILDISH THAN YOU'D THINK.
KAKON (CLUNK)
KAKON
GAYA (GAB)
GAYA
MIND IF I GO FIRST?
SURE.
HEH-HEH-HEH. I'VE GOT A GREAT IDEA.
TA (TMP)
TA
TA
I HAVE A BAD FEELING ABOUT THIS...

DON'T YOU DARE RUN AWAY.
I TOLD YOU I WON'T!
OH YEAH?
YOU'RE PRETTY GOOD WITH KIDS, SHIMAMURA.

MY LITTLE SISTER NEVER STOPS RUNNING AROUND EITHER. I GUESS I'M PRETTY USED TO IT.
THAT'S PROBABLY WHERE IT COMES FROM.
......
AM I YOUR LITTLE SISTER TOO?
HA HA!
CALL ME ONEE-CHAN IF YOU LIKE!
JUST KIDDING.
HUH?
BOSO (WHISPER)
......ONEE-CHAN.
WH-WHAT IS IT, DEAR SISTER?

TA (TMP)
TA
TA
ZUSAAA (SLIDE)
GORO GORO (ROLL)
GO (BONK)
GO
GO
DID I HIT THE MARK?
YEAH, I GUESS.
BUT WHY'D YOU THROW IT LIKE THAT?
I THOUGHT GETTING AS CLOSE AS POSSIBLE WOULD WORK TO MY ADVANTAGE.
...SO SHE'S NOT DUMB. MAYBE SHE JUST HAS NO COMMON SENSE.

DO YOU WANNA GO NEXT, ADACHI?
I'M GOOD.
PUI (SNUB)
GO GET 'EM!
BA— (SHOVE)
BY THE WAY, DO WE GET ANY KIND OF REWARD IF WE WIN THIS COMPETITION?
IF YOU WIN...
...YOU GET ALL PUMPED...
...AND GET TO GO LIKE, "I DID IT! YIPPEE!" RIGHT?

WELL, I LIKE YOU, SHIMAMURA-SAN...
...SO I WOULDN'T FEEL ANY JOY IN BEATING YOU.
GO (THUD)
ACK!
OH......?
THANKS, I GUESS?

THEN...
...I CHALLENGE YOU TO A DUEL.
OH HO!
THINK YOU'VE GOT WHAT IT TAKES TO BEAT MY PRO BOWLING SKILLS?
OF COURSE. YOU'RE GOING DOWN.

WHO ARE YOU ROOTING FOR, SHIMAMURA?
WHAA...?
YEAH, WHO'S IT GONNA BE?
I MAY BE GOOD AT TAKING CARE OF PEOPLE...
...BUT THAT'S JUST ON THE SURFACE.
MAYBE THAT'S WHY WHENEVER SOMEONE TRIES TO GET CLOSE TO ME OR STARTS TO LIKE ME...
...IT MAKES ME WANT TO PUT MY GUARD UP EVEN MORE.
SHIMAMURA-SAN.
SHIMA-MURA.
I GET THIS URGE TO CURL UP IN A BALL ON THE GROUND...
...AND JUST RUN AWAY.

AND YET, HERE I AM.
OKAY, OKAY.
ADACHI, WHAT DO YOU WANT? MY TREAT.
DO YOU SEE ANY MINERAL WATER?
NOT IN A CAN. YOU OKAY WITH POCARI?
HMM, OKAY.

THANKS FOR TODAY.
DID YOU HAVE FUN?
......I GUESS...
キイ
KII (CREAK)

...OKAY, SO?
?
OH, UM, YOU JUST KEPT LOOKING AT ME TODAY.
I THOUGHT MAYBE YOU HAD SOME-THING ON YOUR MIND.
WAS I STARING THAT MUCH?
YUP.

I'M PROBABLY JUST IMAGINING IT, BUT...
...I FEEL LIKE OUR EYES MET A BUNCH OF TIMES.
JUST LIKE THAT.

WOULD YOU...
...PAT MY HEAD FOR A BIT?
HMM.

FUWA (SOFT)
YOU REALLY ARE SUCH A PAMPERED LITTLE GIRL.

A LITTLE MORE?
KOKUN (NOD)
WHY AM I SO HAPPY GETTING MY HEAD PAT BY A GIRL MY AGE?
WHAT'S WRONG WITH ME?
AM I AN IDIOT? AM I JUST WEIRD?
YOU GOOD?
......MM-HMM.
JUST DON'T CALL ME ONEE-CHAN IN CLASS, OKAY?

GIVE ME YOURS. I'LL THROW THEM BOTH OUT.
OH, I'VE STILL GOT SOME LEFT.
I'LL FINISH IT ON THE WAY HOME.
OKAY.
I CAN'T BELIEVE I WANT TO TAKE IT HOME AND PUT IT ON DISPLAY.
I GROSS MYSELF OUT.
BUT ONE GIRL'S TRASH IS ANOTHER GIRL'S TREASURE.

I JUST WANT TO BE SPECIAL TO SHIMAMURA.
AND. I DON'T MEAN THAT IN ANY WEIRD WAY. I REALLY DON'T.
AT THE SAME TIME, AS LONG AS I GET TO BE CLOSE TO HER, I DON'T MIND IF IT DOES GET WEIRD.
SO THAT MEANS...
...I DO LIKE HER...
...IS WHAT I REALIZED.

CONGRATULATIONS
ON THE FIRST VOLUME
GOING ON SALE!
仲谷 鳰
NIO NAKATANI
SLO-MO
VIDEO
PHOTO
SQUARE
PANORAM

NICE TO MEET YOU! MY NAME IS MOKE YUZUHARA.
THANK YOU VERY MUCH FOR PICKING UP THE FIRST VOLUME OF ADACHI AND SHIMAMURA, THE MANGA!
ススス SU SU SU (HOP)
THE OFFER TO TAKE ON THIS SERIES CAME OUT OF THE BLUE—
Moke-san, want to do a manga adaptation?
HUH!?
TRAIN STATION
I LOST A LOT OF SLEEP AT FIRST WITH ALL THE THINGS GOING THROUGH MY MIND, BUT...
MY FIRST SERIALIZATION...
...A MANGA ADAPTATION...
GIN (STARE)
...I FINALLY COMPLETED THE FIRST VOLUME THANKS TO THE SUPPORT I RECEIVED FROM SO MANY PEOPLE.
THANK YOU ALL VERY MUCH!
· Hitoma Iruma-sensei
· My editor
· My designer
· All our collaborators
· All my readers
Special thanks: Nio Nakatani-sensei
PEKORI (BOW)
ONE OF THE MOST DIFFICULT CHALLENGES IN ADAPTING THIS SERIES...
...WAS THAT THERE WAS NO WAY I COULD INCORPORATE EVERYTHING FROM THE ORIGINAL WORK INTO THE MANGA...
BUTSU (MUTTER)
I DON'T HAVE ENOUGH PAGES...
BUT IF I TAKE THIS PART OUT, YOU WON'T GET THE FULL DEPTH OF THIS CHARACTER...
BUTSU
I HAD TO TEARFULLY PART WITH SO MANY SCENES...
...BUT TO MY GREAT RELIEF, IRUMA-SENSEI, THE AUTHOR OF THE ORIGINAL WORK, GAVE ME FREEDOM TO DEPICT THE SERIES AS I SAW FIT.
I AM FOREVER GRATEFUL FOR YOUR SUPPORT, SENSEI.
Iruma-Sensei
I'M GOING TO DO MY BEST TO ENSURE FANS OF THE ORIGINAL WORK AS WELL AS ANY NEWCOMERS ENJOY THIS MANGA...
...SO I'LL BE HAPPY IF YOU CONTINUE TO SUPPORT AND READ THE SERIES!
MOKE YUZUHARA
Twitter @moke14

Adachi and Shimamura ①

ART: **Moke Yuzuhara** ORIGINAL STORY: **Hitoma Iruma** CHARACTER DESIGN: **Non**

Translation: Alexandra McCullough-Garcia
Lettering: Alexis Eckerman

Yen Press
150 West 30th Street, 19th Floor
New York, NY 10001

Visit us at yenpress.com

facebook.com/yenpress
twitter.com/yenpress
yenpress.tumblr.com
instagram.com/yenpress

First Yen Press Edition: January 2021

Yen Press is an imprint of Yen Press, LLC.
The Yen Press name and logo are trademarks of Yen Press, LLC.

The publisher is not responsible for websites (or their content) that are not owned by the publisher.

Library of Congress Control Number: 2020948852

ISBNs: 978-1-9753-2003-4 (paperback)
978-1-9753-2004-1 (ebook)

10 9 8 7 6 5 4 3 2 1

WOR

Printed in the United States of America

You're reading the wrong way!

Turn to the back of the book
for an original short story
by Hitoma Iruma!

came pouring in.

"I mean...you'll probably need the handicap," she shot back boldly, lowering her eyes and smirking. Maybe she had some confidence in her game. She had been the one to suggest the match, after all. At any rate, it wasn't like I had the total upper hand. Specifically, my back and head were burning up. Summer should have been long gone, so what was the deal with this heat?

Was there someone focusing all the sunlight on my back with a magnifying glass or something?

I twirled my hair through my fingers as I turned around to check. I heard the ball plunk across the table but decided not to let it get to me and allowed myself to feel drawn to the light.

Sheltered in this dark enclave, I looked up toward something brighter. I gazed off into the distance as if longing for something in a sea of contradiction. The clouds standing in for the sky spoke to me of the season and the wind.

"Shimamura, that's one point for me, you know."

At Adachi's words, I finally turned back around.

I looked over in the direction she was pointing as if to say "There, over there," and saw a colorful Ping-Pong ball bouncing its way toward the wall. I ran after it, caught it, and let out a "Haaah!" as I struck a dramatic pose. Adachi took one look at me twirling the racket and passing it back and forth between my hands, laughed, and said, "Weirdo."

Maybe it wouldn't be so bad to get a bit weird. A little change might do me some good. Weird, huh... All right, I'll show you weird. I don't know how, but I'm going to try a curveball.

I balanced the Ping-Pong ball in the palm of my hand and cleared my head. A stream of cicadas' cries continued to float in from the outside world, carrying with them the last afterglows of summer.

We were classmates after all, and we had both wandered into the same hiding spot of all places. We probably saw things in similar ways, which made sense. Could that be why it never felt like a chore to be around her? A little late in the game, but the reason I liked being here finally dawned on me.

The range she chose to move in also felt right for some reason. She didn't force herself to go all the way outside or even to the first floor of the gym. Instead, she reached out to the table right in front of us, like... I can't really explain it, but that level of energy was on point.

I liked those things about her.

"But, um, we don't have to if you don't want to."

Adachi started to pull back the offer; I'd taken too long to answer. It would have been easy to brush it off as too much work, just like always. But I'd already gotten up, so I thought I might as well try. People trip on the tiniest pebbles and walk miles over a lost game of rock, paper, scissors all the time. There doesn't always have to be a big reason to do something.

"Could be fun."

Anything to keep boredom from taking over our sanctuary. Maybe passing a Ping-Pong ball between us wouldn't be so bad.

"Whoa, it's so sticky."

"Ew, you're right."

We commented on how the long-abandoned rackets felt in our hands as we took our places across the table from each other. Adachi went over to the side closest to the gym and I stood with my back to the windows.

"Heh-heh-heh. Kinda bright, huh?" I snickered, pleased with my choice to put the sun behind me. Adachi's face flashed with recognition once she saw my battle plan, and her eyes narrowed. Her eyelashes quivered as they tried to shield her from the sunlight that

Our school didn't even have a Ping-Pong club anymore. If it did, I may not have met Adachi at all.

Adachi stood up. I thought maybe she'd head home, but she left her shoes where they were. Plus, she didn't head for the exit and instead came closer to the corner of the gym. I wondered what had gotten into her and absentmindedly watched as she lifted a cardboard box. She wrapped her arms around it and carried it back over to me.

"What's that?"

"Paddles and balls and stuff."

"Paddles?"

Adachi started taking out the items in the box and lining them up on the table. I stood, curious, and saw rackets and balls, just like she'd said. It was all Ping-Pong equipment. There was a net, the hardware, and everything else you'd need to play. A cloud of dust came rising up from the box that must have sat unused for ages. I started to choke even before breathing any of it in. Adachi finished laying everything out as I stood there waving the dust away and said, "Hey, want to play table tennis?"

"...You mean Ping-Pong?" I asked.

"Why'd you use the trademarked name?"

"No reason... Actually, I didn't even know it was trademarked."

I'd thought that was just what everyone called it. I was impressed, but Adachi started to doubt herself and said, "I guess."

Pretty much what you could expect from two borderline dropouts. But we can put that aside for now.

I thought the suggestion was a bit unusual for Adachi. Or actually, suggesting anything at all, much less the idea of moving, felt unexpected. I also doubted whether I knew Adachi well enough to tell what counted as unusual, but we can put that aside too.

Maybe Adachi picked up the same vibes and chose to move.

"How about you, Shimamura?" she asked me back, almost out of obligation.

"Yeah, they found out. They've been giving me grief about it ever since." I didn't even get lunch made for me anymore. And they hated my hair, even though I'd been so excited to dye it.

"Huh..."

The conversation died off with her single, somewhat indifferent response. That's how it always went.

Well, I guess I'd go back to class if I wanted a fun, lively chat with a classmate anyway.

We fell silent. But not like in winter when sounds fade into the snow; the space around my ears felt heavy. Like the sounds hadn't gone far out of their reach, but they were pretending not to notice. Yet it wasn't exactly a tranquil silence. It grated on my nerves. I pinched and pulled the hem of my skirt and breathed a heavy sigh.

"Well, whatever," I started to say, but then gave up.

Being there wasn't exactly uncomfortable, but I was afraid I might get kicked out again if I just sat and did nothing. Not by a teacher, but by a much greater nuisance. Yes, boredom might come knocking.

Boredom festers in idleness.

By definition, lingering anywhere means you abandon any kind of flow. Water pools and muddies around you as you sink down, down to the depths. And if you don't want that to happen, all you can do is move, even if it means tugging at a pulley that won't get you anywhere.

I lifted my head up as those thoughts passed through my mind, and my eyes landed on the legs of a Ping-Pong table standing quietly in the room. It was folded out and ready to use but may as well have already been thrown in the trash. No one ever came by to touch it.

It was here in this suspended space and time that I first met Adachi.

In the dying days of summer, new meetings are steeped in a certain listless energy. The two of us lingered in the gym like moss clinging to a rock.

"Hey, Adachi."

"Yeah?"

The warm air dried up the back of my throat as I opened my mouth to breathe it in. It felt like so much trouble to get up and try to quench that thirst. Maybe that's why we didn't talk much. We were model slackers in every sense of the word.

"Do your parents know you cut class?"

The question came to me randomly. I floated it over to Adachi, who turned her eyes away toward the wall.

"Dunno... We almost never talk at home," she mumbled, her voice devoid of any interest. It was as if she was watching the scene from a distance, her lifeless eyes merely following along... Like it was hardly worth thinking about. Maybe she didn't really have a tight relationship with her family. We spent a lot of time together, but we didn't ever talk about such things, so I never got even the tiniest bit closer to knowing what home life was like for her. Not that I felt any strong desire to find out.

We shared the same space, but that's all there was to it. Like a couple of fish kept in the same tank. We have one at home with some fish that my little sister looks after.

...But do fish actually think nothing of the others in there with them? Do they really feel no urge to get along and be friends? I guess I'll never see far enough in to read their minds, no matter how much I peer into their tank.

Adac
and
Shimamura
0.99

By Hitoma Iruma
Illustration by Moke Yuzuhara

I thought I was basically an adult when I first entered middle school. Obviously, I was a little off, but that's when I realized I'm not much of a people person. Or maybe that's just what I convinced myself so I could run away and never have to deal with the things that annoyed me.

And now here I was, a high school student with pretty bleak prospects of ever actually growing up, seeking shelter on the second floor of the school gym from the packed classroom, its lessons meant to prepare us for our shining futures, and the sight of my classmates looking prim and proper, seated in those boxy chairs.

Here, the ceiling stood between me and the sky that should have already left summer behind and trapped hot, humid air beneath it. This heat would bud deep inside my uniform at the slightest shrug of my shoulders, leaving me in a perpetually uncomfortable state. Ever since I stopped going to class, I got this surreal sense that I had somehow brought even the seasons to a standstill. Coarse, dusty particles grazed my fingers as I traced them along the parts of the floor that mops and brooms never reached.